CONTAINER GARDENING VEGETABLES:

A Complete Guide to Grow Your Urban Garden and Have a Rewarding Activity

TAMMY SOLOMON & CLOE WYLIE

Table Of Contents

Introduction

Container gardening practice allows you to garden all year round irrespective of your outdoor climate. Plants grown in containers are more accessible, given little chance to weeds, and require the use of fewer gardening tools. You can rearrange them in a way that suits your taste and needs.

If you cannot grow a vegetable garden outside of your home because of poor soil, if you live in a limited space with no access to an outdoor patio, or if you have a small deck. You can still enjoy the simple pleasures that vegetable container gardening offers.

The increasing popularity of container gardens in different parts of the world has taught many people the benefits of cultivating these masterpieces. You might see plants growing in containers on balconies or rooftops, in office spaces, restaurants, and more. People can create special gardens—regardless of the location or the area available to them. Additionally, individuals find they can grow special plants that may require extra attention concerning soil and water—plants they could not manage if they were part of a large garden.

Vegetable Container Gardening offers the option of allowing you to own a garden. It gives you the flexibility to reorder or move your plants around whenever and wherever you like. You also have the freedom to choose the plants you want to grow, whether they are flowers, vegetables, herbs, or combinations of all three. You can even grow tropical plants during the winter months if you keep the plants inside your home. Then, when the summertime comes, you can either transplant your plants outside or simply move the containers outdoors.

Creating a Vegetable container garden makes it possible for those who live in the city to enjoy eating fresh salads with the lettuce, tomatoes, and herbs they have grown. High-rise patios and porches become even more beautiful with the addition of container gardens displaying their arrays of brilliant colors and shapes.

Vegetable gardening in Containers is extremely versatile, is not difficult to achieve, and has many advantages.

A container vegetable garden could provide pleasure and fresh vegetables. A well-drained growing medium, sufficient water and fertilizer, and plenty of sunlight are essential to make the garden productive. Just ensure you water your garden almost every day, because if the plants dry out thoroughly around watering, this may lead the plants to drop off their fruit or flowers. You might also want to use fertilizer every few weeks.

The primary purpose of container gardening merely relies on the selection of choices made by the gardener.

In this book, I want to take the practice of container gardening and concentrate on growing vegetables in them. If you read my book on container gardening, you will be familiar with what is discussed in the succeeding chapters. I encourage you to read through the material presented here, even if you have read my other book because there will be some things you may not remember from my other book. You will discover new information I have included in this one. Ultimately, I want this book to be a complete resource for anyone desiring to grow vegetables in containers, so some repetition from my other book is necessary.

CHAPTER 1:

When use this type of gardening

When to use

L iving in the city has its benefits. City dwellers have employment and entertainment options people living in the country simply don't have.

What people living in the city don't have is access to ample open space and fresh air free of smog. They mostly miss out on the ability to spend time one on one with nature in their backyard. Gardening and growing fruit or vegetables are one of the many things city-dwellers forgo for the convenience of living in the city. They think that since they're living in cramped quarters with little open dirt available to plant crops on that, they have to forget all about growing their produce.

What many people in the city don't realize is container gardening allows aspiring gardeners to grow plants in areas where it would otherwise be impossible to plant seeds and grow them into plants. Lack of fertile soil or a plot of land on which to plant seeds is no longer a valid excuse thanks to container gardening. This innovative form of gardening allows you to create a garden in almost any setting imaginable, as long as there are light and access to water.

If you have limited space, container gardening allows you to grow plants pretty much anywhere you can fit a container. The container doesn't have to be big. A head of lettuce can be grown in a colander. This means you can grow plants in your home, on your patio or balcony, and even on your desk at work. No matter where you are, no matter where you live, no matter how cramped for space you are. You can enjoy a small slice of what nature has to offer by taking advantage of container gardening. It's like having your own little natural oasis in an otherwise bland and infertile setting.

Container gardening allows those living in condos, apartment buildings, and other areas with a lack of access to a plot of fertile land to grow small yet surprisingly productive crops of produce, plants, and flowers using what little space they have. It also gives people who live in areas where the ground soil is polluted to grow plants that never touch the soil. As long as you can free up space for a pot or two, you have room for a container garden. That's all the space you're going to need. I've seen plants grown in containers in windowsills, hanging from terraces and even placed on fire escapes. Where there's a will, there's a way, and people are continually coming up with new ideas for container gardening.

A growing number of people are successfully growing produce at home in containers. This book provides you with the information you need to join their ranks. You can use container gardening to supplement your meals with healthy home-grown vegetables and herbs that taste better and contain fewer toxins than the produce grown commercially.

Container gardening is the perfect solution to this problem, allowing you to grow vegetables, fruit, flowers, and herbs no matter where you live. It is very easy to turn container gardening into a feature that can be eye-catching and attractive, plus you can plant on walls or fences rather than just putting containers on the floor.

But container gardening isn't just limited to urban dwellers, even for people with gardens, container gardening is a great way to maximize your usage of space, grow extra plants or also to grow plants that wouldn't normally thrive in your area. You can plant up the container and leave it in the sun outside during the summer months, but as it gets colder, you can move the container indoors to protect your delicate plant from the elements.

Containers are very flexible, and you can grow a wide variety of different plants in them, and you will learn not only what you can plant but also what you should not plant in containers. Plus, you will get more in-depth information about some of the more popular plants you can grow in containers and specific advice about them.

Feeding and watering your containers is extremely important, and it has to be done right so you will find out more about how to do this properly so that your plants thrive. You will also find out what to do with your containers over the winter months, another critical and often forgotten subject.

Modern cities have evolved over the last couple of hundreds of years, and during that period, the land on which they are built has been subjected to a wide range of uses. Cities continuously evolve, and regulations relating to the urban environment do likewise. Unfortunately, pollution and land use regulations were not, in the past, quite what they were today. The legacy that this has left for us is not always the healthiest one, and, in particular, the soil beneath our city streets may contain significant traces of many contaminants, including dangerous heavy metals. The good news is that container gardening helps the urban gardener to sidestep this potentially dangerous form of pollution.

Water pollution is not as easy to avoid even when container gardening, and although a great source of water for your containers is the public supply, this is often chlorinated. Plants do not always react well to chlorinated water, and many gardeners are concerned by the effect on productivity that this has. Rainwater provides a viable solution, and plants will benefit from nutrients found naturally within it. The ambient temperature of rain, as it falls or from storage within the garden, is also better for the plants themselves. Additionally, although there will inevitably be pollutants in rainwater gathered from the atmosphere, pollutants are filtered out naturally by the soil. Generally, it is accepted that the air pollutants found in the rain are diluted to a high degree and will pose no threat to health. When storing water on site, it is important to ensure storage is in opaque containers, and nets are placed over barrels or tanks to ensure mosquitoes and other insect life. Harvesting rainwater for gardening is also a recognized benefit for the environment in general, reducing the pressure on public wastewater operations, sewers, and drains. The impact can be particularly significant in urban environments prone to severe flooding.

Air pollution can be high in urban areas, and the location of your garden may well mean that this can be a significant concern. Close to busy highways, or in very built-up areas (rooftop gardens in particular), the levels of pollution in the air may be high. However, these pollutants will only be found on the plants themselves. For consumption, it's wise to ensure that produce is properly washed before cooking or eating. Air pollution affects most plants, but in reality, these pollutants can be washed away, and, unlike commercially produced food, you stand a good chance of understanding what contaminants are in the atmosphere where you grow the food itself!

The Benefits of Container Gardening

Container gardening is a great way to learn the ins and outs of gardening without having to grow plants on a massive scale. While the vast majority of container gardeners do so because of space constraints, a growing number of people living outside of the city are realizing container gardening may be the way to go, especially when they're first starting to grow plants. When you confine your plants to a container, you eliminate (or at least lessen) the effects of many common problems gardeners have.

Container gardening has the following benefits when compared to regular gardening:

<u>You can garden anywhere</u>

You can set a container anywhere you have space. While this may seem restrictive at first, keep in mind that containers don't have to be huge. Baskets, pots, jars, and anything else you can put dirt in can be placed on the ground, mounted to walls or hung from the ceiling to create a garden. You aren't limited to gardening in a patch of dirt or a planter box in your yard. You can garden wherever you'd like, indoors or out.

Your containers are mobile

Is there a big storm or a deep freeze looming? Container gardening allows you the freedom to move all but the largest of containers inside to get them out of the elements. You're no longer at the mercy of Mother Nature. You can move your containers around to take advantage of the sun and the rain, and you can bring them inside when the weather takes a turn for the worse.

You can keep your crops safe from animals

If you live in an area where rodents, rabbits, or even deer have been known to sneak into the garden at night and make a snack of growing produce, you can set up a system that mainly protects your garden from these pests. Root-nibbling animals are also blocked because they aren't able to dig through the bottom of the container your plants are stored in. Hanging a container or bringing it in at night will protect your plants from larger animals.

You choose the amount of light your plants get

When you plant something in the ground, you're at the mercy of the movement of the sun. Houses, buildings, fences, and all sorts of other structures play a crucial role in how much sun the crops you plant are going to get. With container gardening, you can plant something that needs a lot of sunlight in a place where it's most likely to get the sunlight it needs, be it on your deck, on the roof of your building, or hanging from a window outside your apartment. Containers can be moved throughout the day to ensure they get the right amount of light.

You bring the outside inside

Living in the city can be a rather dreary life, especially if you spend a lot of time in the industrial areas of town. Coming home to a container garden rife with living, breathing plants can provide a means of escaping the daily grind while you take time out to attend to your plants.

You can tailor your garden to suit your style

Pick containers and plants that match up with your personality and lifestyle. You can sparsely populate your home or balcony with a few understated containers, or you can go all out and create a veritable jungle of exciting and colorful plants and containers. No matter what your style is, you should be able to find a container/plant combination that fits your needs.

You can garden year-round, no matter what the weather

With container gardening, you're no longer limited to gardening during the warm summer months. When things outside are cold, grey, and dreary, you can have a beautiful group of plants growing indoors. This gives you the freedom to grow to produce out of season.

Gardening at Your Convenient Time

The urge for gardening depends on the weather most times, where a good number of gardeners prefer to garden at the beginning of the planting seasons. The time of growing your plants usually depends on your geographical location. Considering the temperate regions, for example, you will have to garden as the winter approaches and the frozen ground wipes off the surface of the earth. While when it comes to the tropics, planting is executed at the starting of the rainy season.

It is an Easy Gardening Method for Beginners

In traditional gardening, some specific factors will typically occur, for example, weeds that have seeds that grow faster than the very plants' seeds we intend to grow. That is the reason why most of the experienced gardeners dedicate more energy and time to prepare their vegetable bed. If you plant your garden with less preparation, you will be at the risk of having your beds overrun with weeds in no time. And this can be quite discouraging, especially to beginners.

Elimination of Space Constraints

People living in high rise apartments or townhouses are usually faced with space constraint issues, especially when it comes to in-ground gardening because they mostly don't have outdoor spaces to call their own. Fortunately, if it is pot gardening, all these shouldn't be a problem.

Bringing Gardening Indoors

Container gardening allows you to grow hundreds of houseplants that will conveniently grow indoors, especially when planted close to a sunny window. Fruits and vegetables can be grown under the right conditions when they are being exposed to sufficient sunlight, and even in the absence of the sun. Artificial lighting can also be used.

A lesser Amount of Water is required

Container gardening requires less water when compared to traditional gardening. In regular gardening, when you provide enough water to the plants, the water will end up spreading to the surrounding soil. And water will evaporate quickly due to the larger surface area of the land, causing it to dry off quickly, thus call for more watering.

Easier Pests and Diseases Control

The control of pests and disease is a major concern in gardening generally, especially in-ground traditional gardening. Failure to control pests and conditions will result in poor harvest or complete loss of the affected plants. The risk of this is, however, very minimal in container gardening as the effect of pests can easily be noticed and hence, controlled before it becomes a major problem. Pests and disease control in container gardening usually require little or no chemical application. It makes the harvest almost always chemical-free. In dealing with the pests, cotton buds soaked in rubbing alcohol can be used to eliminate pests like aphids, while brush can be used to remove larger insects.

The Growth of Weed Is Limited in Container Gardening

One of the disadvantages of traditional gardening is, having to put up with the weeds. It is very limited in the container if at all, it is experienced. It can also be quickly addressed without having to use toxic chemicals, which could affect the growing plants. Container gardening is, therefore, a suitable method not just for experienced gardeners but also for those with little or no experience.

Soil can be adjusted according to plants' requirements

If you live in a place where the quality of soil is poor, it might be impossible to grow and harvest plants successfully, but with container gardening, you can easily buy soil or create a soil mix that your plant will fruitfully grow in. Also, if the plants you wish to plant have different soil requirements, then you can simply place them in separate containers and fill the containers with the correct soil types.

Weeding will be much easier

Because your plants are enclosed and contained in containers, weeding will be much easier and not much work.

Confines wild-growing plants

When wild-growing plants are freely planted in a garden, they can sometimes cause problems, as they tend to overtake other plants and grow in different places. With container gardening, however, this is not a problem, as the containers can enclose and contain the plant. If the plants grow too big for their containers, you can decide to transfer the plants and submerge them in your garden without removing them from their containers.

Protects plants from wild animals

If there are wild animals in the place where you live, plants planted in your garden might get destroyed or eaten. To avoid this, you can start an indoor garden instead.

Watering will be easier

Different plants have different water requirements. If you plant to grow various plants, watering will be much easier because you can simply water them individually without the hassle.

Bringing them with you is easy

If you frequently move to a new house or travel, container gardening is ideal. Since they are in containers, you can effortlessly bring them with you without putting pressure or them and without stressing them out.

Moving them around will be effortless

Just like water requirements, different plants have different sunlight requirements too. One of the best things about growing plants in container gardens is that you can quickly move them around your house to make sure that they get the right amount of sunlight that they need. If it's winter season, you can follow the sun and place them in an area where the sun shines best, or if it's summer season and the sun gets too hot, you can relocate them to a place where there is partial shade.

CHAPTER 2:

Planning Your Container Garden

N othing beats the feeling of getting to use your herbs and vegetables, and even flowers, straight from your garden. There is a wide variety of plants that can be planted and grown in a container garden. With the right amount of planning, you can easily grow just about any type of plant you choose, given that their living conditions are met, of course.

Plan which plants to grow. Plants have specific requirements that need to be met for them to grow correctly. Therefore, you cannot just plant whichever plant you desire. You have to take into consideration the weather, climate, and overall environment of where you live. Make a list of plants you want to grow and check their sun, water, and soil requirements.

Evaluate your house. Before you buy seeds or seedlings, carefully evaluate your home. Determine the areas which get the most sunlight, count how many hours the sunlight shines on those areas, and identify the places which are partially shaded. Once you have listed those down, compare the requirements of the plants that you wish to grow and choose accordingly.

Determine where to place the plants. If the area in your house which gets the most sun does not have enough space, choose to hang your containers or create shelves to place your plants on. These steps are very important, especially if you plan to expand your indoor garden in the future. You can also choose to set your plants somewhere else and then move them outside to get some sunlight; however, the constant moving may stress them out, which can hinder their growth.

Some of the most fundamental questions to ask you include but are not limited to the following

Where will I site my raised bed garden?

What type of raised gardens will I adopt?

What do I plant?

When do I plant?

What do I do about weeds?

Do I need to set up irrigation?

Where will I site my raised bed garden?

Plants and vegetables are never going to survive for long without sunlight. It is an essential part of their diet. The more the sunshine, the higher the tendency for your garden to flourish. On average, plants need about eight hours of sunlight daily. So, this means your choice of location is highly dependent on where in your yard receives the most amount of the sun.

Another thing to consider in locating your raised bed gardens is the type of soil you have present within your yard. As much as you can import a whole lot of compost soil from outside, it is crucial to see if the ground within your space is usable for such an exercise. This test will help cut down costs and will ease incorporation. So, in an event where you find out that your yard indeed has a significant amount of soil that will adequately support plant life, it would be a shame if you don't use them. Please ensure that before you use the soil from your yard for planting within the frames, and that it is entirely rid of weeds, grasses, and debris that won't impede plant growth.

If your number of besteads is much, then buying soil in large amounts will suffice. They come in a cubic foot, cubic yard or cubic meter. When making your purchase, you can demand about sixty percent topsoil, thirty percent compost, and about ten percent potting soil, which contains essential plant nutrients contained in perlite, vermiculite, and peat moss.

There are other options to explore in the case where finding quality soil is hard to come by. A mixture of compost and potting soil at equal proportions will serve wonderfully.

What type of raised gardens will I adopt?

You would have to go through the three types of raised beds gardening earlier and make your choice. They all have their unique characteristics, which can be customized to meet your preferred demands for your yard.

What do I plant?

Your choice of what to plant will significantly influence other critical decisions about your chosen adventure.

First, make up your mind on whether you would be planting for aesthetics or consumption. Planting for aesthetics will require that you consider the type of materials to use, how high above the ground, and the variety of shapes to employ. Planting for consumption, on the other hand, will require a particular focus on soil type, depth, and sizes of bedsteads.

In both cases, you are encouraged to choose out of a pool of your favorite plants. Plant to what you love to eat-tomatoes, peppers, potatoes, cucumbers, _etc._ you can choose to have a mixture of consumption and beautiful plants. Just ensure that you don't plant them tightly together, as this will increase competition for nutrients and air circulation.

You must research on the growing habits of the plants you choose. Some are crawlers, and others are climbers. Some are root plants, while others are tubers. Read up on your preferred choices. Also, you must read up on which plants would be right to grow together. While planting tomatoes with cabbages is fine, planting tomatoes with crawling cucumbers can prove to be challenging.

Finally, do your research on how to effectively grow your plant, taking into cognizance the prevailing climate within your region. Some plants may not need to be planted from seed level in your garden because the favorable weather which they may require might be gone long before they reach harvest. So, it would be best to purchase them from a nursery and transplant. In any case, the onus is on you to do thorough research before making your choices and proceeding to plant.

When do I plant?

This question is an important one. Your answer will be determined your choice of plants, the current climate within your region, and at what level you choose to do your planting.

Some plants thrive in cold weather; broccoli, for example, but tomatoes will die out in such cold temperatures. With each plant, there are the best times to plant them. You must do your research and put down frost dates and take note of soil temperatures. Under no condition should you grow any plant that is averse to cold when the frost hasn't passed?

As some plants are opposed to low temperatures, so are others that can't survive in extreme temperatures. Be careful to figure out what your garden choices may require. On average, most plants do well in reasonable soil temperatures of between sixty to seventy degrees Fahrenheit.

In the event where you embark on transplanting, you must do so when temperatures are average, and the weather is just right. In the case where you transplant and the weather turns out to be harsh, then you'll have to cover them up for the meantime and shield them from intense sunlight and dry winds.

What do I do about weeds?

Weeds can be an inconvenience. They are unwanted plants that grow anywhere they can. They are not only undesirable, unappealing to the eyes, but they also compete with your planted crops for soil nutrients and space.

It's essential to get rid of weeds before you embark on constructing your couches. These weeds can be weeded out using simple garden took like hoes and hand trowels. Weeds can also be eliminated by using soil and environmentally friendly pesticides. These should be applied as instructed by the manufacturer and within specified periods as prescribed.

In the case where you import topsoil, compost, and peat moss for mixture and eventual installing into the bedsteads, you must ensure that seeds, plants, and roots of unwanted plants are entirely removed.

Do I need to set up irrigation?

In most cases, yes, you would. Irrigation is vital for your plant to thrive. Without water, plants will dehydrate and wither away. Unless you live in a region where it rains throughout the year, you will need to have a plan on how to water your plants. If your garden is small, then watering it with a watering can be done as often as required. But in the case where your garden is quite large and manually watering each bedstead every day without breaking down is nearly impossible. You will need to put up irrigation mechanisms. Simple piping done by a qualified plumber will go a long way in handling the challenge. Ensure that the plumbing work is done before the bedsteads are laid. That way, it will be easier to co-opt into the entire arrangement. Also, consider collecting rainwater as it will significantly reduce your spending cost on water.

With the above questions answered, embarking on raised bed gardening should be a remarkable experience for you. As you journey through each step, you will have more questions. You need to concentrate on the project while seeking further clarification as you go on. Listed below are some points for you to read and take note of as they are essential.

Other Tips

Don't step on the prepared soil, ever.

Plant, then mulch.

Install irrigation mechanisms before laying the beds

Put in place barricades against the creeping in of weeds.

Have a yearly compost dressing of the beds.

Keep the topsoil as fleecy as possible.

Have a plan to plant cover crops.

Never neglect the soil, even if you are not gardening.

Research on your choice plants, never presumes you know them.

Maintenance is critical; don't sleep on it.

Designing Your Container Garden

There are several ways you can design a container garden. Be creative and design a garden suited to your individual needs, and you'll be much more likely to enjoy the time you spend taking care of it.

You can choose the plants you want to grow and plan the location and containers according to the plant types you've picked, or you can select the containers first, and then make a decision as to what you're going to plant in them. There are entire books and websites dedicated to container garden design alone. The only limitations are the bounds of your imagination—or the bounds of other people's vision if you peruse the available literature.

The first consideration you're going to have to make is whether you want a functional container garden that provides you with products or whether you're going for something that looks great but maybe less functional. That's not to say you can't have a garden that both looks amazing and provides you with an abundance of produce. It's just going to take more work and planning.

Location, Location, Location

Where you plan on keeping your containers has a huge bearing on what you're going to be able to plant in them. To successfully plant vegetables, you're going to need to find an area that gets at least 4 hours of direct sunlight, or you're going to need a source of artificial light.

The following areas may get enough sunlight to allow you to grow vegetables using natural sunlight alone:

- ☐ A greenhouse.

- ☐ *Balconies.*

- ☐ Close to glass doors that get direct sunlight.

- ☐ Containers hung outside.

- ☐ Fire escapes.

- ☐ Planter boxes hung from outside windows.

- ☐ Raised beds.

- ☐ The roof of your apartment or office building.

- ☐ Windowsills.

- ☐ Your front porch.

- ☐ Your yard.

Even if you're unable to set a container directly in one area that gets enough light, you may be able to set up a system in which you use foil or another shiny material to reflect light from a nearby sunny area to the area where you're growing your plants. Thinking outside the box allows you to grow plants using natural sunlight in an area that gets little to no direct sunlight. Reflective material like glass, mirrors, and shiny metal can all be used to direct sunlight from a sunnier area to your plants.

CHAPTER 3:

Container to select

How to Choose the Right Pot for Every Plant

In truth, there is no specific or right container to use for container gardening. There are so many containers that you can choose to use. You can decide to use pots, old jugs or cartons, or even watering cans. But to help you choose among hundreds of choices, here are some guidelines that you can follow.

Style of the container

There are hundreds or even thousands of container styles. You can choose to use anything that you want at all. You can grow your plant in a clay pot, a fishbowl, in a shoebox, or even in a trash can. Your choice will be depending on your budget, your design preference, and the type of plant that you wish to grow.

Size of the container. Of course, the larger the box, the higher the chance that your plants will grow healthy and strong. The advantage of using larger pots is that you need to water less frequently because the more soil there is, the longer the moisture will be held. However, if your space is limited, then you need to consider planting smaller plants that can survive in a limited space.

Self-watering container

If you frequently travel or want a container garden but do not have that much time to tend to it, you can purchase a self-watering box to make sure that your plants get watered regularly. A self-watering container is very convenient to own. Still, if you live in an area where it mostly rains, you might have to monitor your plants more closely to make sure that they do not drown and die.

Drainage. As mentioned earlier, you can choose to use any container that you want. Still, you have to make sure that it has holes for drainage, or it is a material that you can easily make holes to.

The ideal container for growing vegetables, in particular, should be deep enough to allow your plants to develop a strong root system. Also, the container should have a minimum diameter of 24 inches.

You can either buy new containers, or you can use existing ones that are lying around your home. Terra-cotta containers are generally considered good choices, but you can also re-use your old plastic trash bins by creating drainage holes in the base to turn them into pots. To maximize space, you can also consider using hanging containers.

Attractive-looking containers are very inspiring and motivating, which is why you might like to consider using glazed ceramic planters. The great thing about them is that the material is porous, which will allow the roots of your plants to have access to air. If this sounds too fancy, you can substitute with a polypropylene pot.

Each type of container has its pros and cons. For instance, clay or terra-cotta can break easily, especially by frost. Avoid using them if you live in the northern areas.

Cast concrete is very durable, except they are also very heavy and unsuitable for decks or balconies. Metal containers are durable as well, but they are heat conductors, which can damage your plants' roots. If you choose to use them, line them with plastic first.

Plastic and fiberglass containers are also sturdy and cheap, but make sure not to choose thin ones as these will become brittle and would eventually break.

Wooden containers look great and can protect the roots of your plants from fluctuating temperature changes. Pick only the rot-resistant variety such as locust, cedar, or pine treated with a non-toxic preservative.

Choosing a container should be easy. All you need is something that holds dirt and has holes in the bottom for excess water to drain out of. Easy enough, right?

The problem isn't finding the right container; it's picking from the plethora of proper containers available today. There are tens of thousands of containers out there, and most of them will do a decent job. You can go with ordinary containers and pots designed for container gardening, or you can get creative and use something that wasn't designed to grow vegetables in. The fact of the matter is you can grow vegetables in pretty much anything that holds dirt.

Here are some items people commonly use to grow vegetables in:

- Antique cans and containers.

- *Boots.*

- Buckets.

- Coffee cans.

- *Colanders.*

- Concrete pots.

- Custom-made containers.

- Designer containers.

- Enamelware.

- Fountains.

- ☐ Glassware.

- ☐ Hanging containers.

- ☐ Ice chests.

- ☐ Laundry baskets.

- ☐ Metal pots.

- ☐ Metal troughs.

- ☐ Old oil cans.

- ☐ Pans.

- ☐ Pedestals.

- ☐ Plastic containers.

- ☐ *Pots.*

- ☐ Terra cotta pots.

- ☐ Toolboxes.

- ☐ *Trashcans.*

- ☐ *Urns.*

- ☐ *Vases.*

- ☐ Wash tubs.

- ☐ Water coolers.

- ☐ Watering cans.

- ☐ Wheelbarrows.

- ☐ Window boxes.

- ☐ Wire baskets.

- ☐ Wood crates.

- ☐ Wood or metal boxes.

As you can see, pretty much anything that can hold dirt can be repurposed into a container for container gardening. This allows you to get creative and create containers that are interesting and unique. The material and type of container you use can reflect the style of the area where you're going to keep the container, or you can opt to go with something plain and functional. When you're using unconventional containers, it helps to stick to one theme. You want to create an exciting and unique look, not end up with your house looking like you couldn't control yourself at the local flea market.

Size of the container

Of course, the larger the container, the higher the chance that your plants will grow healthy and strong. The advantage of using larger pots is that you need to water less frequently because the more soil there is, the longer the moisture will be held. However, if your space is limited, then you need to consider planting smaller plants that can survive in a limited space.

Drainage

As mentioned earlier, you can choose to use any container that you want, but you have to make sure that it has holes for drainage, or it is a material that you can easily make holes in.

CHAPTER 4:

Where to Put Your Planter

Where will the container be located?

Light is one of the most important considerations if you want to grow happy, healthy, prolific flowers. Watch the sun and note if the container location is sunny, shady, or partly shaded. Be sure to pick flowers that will thrive in that light.

Is this container going to be a centerpiece point or part of a grouping?

If this container is a stand-alone, "look at me" planting, it will need to be a large outstanding container planted with large foliage and flowers. If it's part of a grouping, you will have more leeway in choosing a variety of plants and containers. If you are planning on grouping your containers, apply the "rule of three." An odd number is always more pleasing when grouping anything, whether it's plants or containers.

What type of home do you have? Is it stately and traditional? Homey and comfortable, a log cabin in the woods, or stucco home in a development?

The containers and flowers you choose should reflect that atmosphere. Look around at various containers in your area. Take photos with your phone while out walking. Look at gardening magazines and take note of the types of vessels and flowers used in areas similar to where you live.

Eventually, you will get a feel for what looks and feels right for you and your environment.

It may seem like common sense, but this is one of the main reasons why farmers do not yield enough crops. You must plan. Know what you want to plant seasons ahead and purchase the necessary seeds and tools to get the harvest started.

You can check online to see when your favorite fruits, veggies, nuts, and herbs are in season. Waiting until that season comes to plant may mean that you won't yield the product you could have if you would have planned it before.

Scheduling is the key yet again when it comes to planting in this way. You must have your crops in the rotation when you are prepping for the year.

Organic agriculture reduces the use of non-renewable sources of energy. It means that you won't be wasting as much of the earth's resources by farming. Growing organic lessens the greenhouse effect and global warming, which is a major issue, especially for those of us who live in the northern hemisphere. It is only possible because growing organic stops carbon from seeping into the atmosphere while it's still in the soil. The increased carbon storage raises productivity because crops that are grown in carbon-rich soil tend to increase agriculture against climate change. It means that organic vegetables have a significantly better chance of surviving our rough climate than non-organic crops.

Make sure you choose the right plants for your location. You won't find papayas growing in most organic areas because the climate isn't right. You can learn which plants will thrive in your garden by checking the USDA's Hardiness Zones.

CHAPTER 5:

How to Choose Soil for Your Planters

What Type of Soil Do I Use?

Having good quality soil is one of the most essential parts of container gardening. The basic purpose of the soil for your containers and plants is to help with the retention of moisture, to support the structure of your plants, to bring air to their roots, and to maintain nutrients necessary for your plant's health.

When choosing to grow vegetation in containers, you will find that your traditional ways of thinking about soil have to change. Container gardening requires soils that can drain well and can aerate well—all while being able to hold on to and retain the moisture necessary for your plants to grow.

The first rule to know when preparing the soil for your containers is this: Do not use regular soil from your yard or garden, even if it looks great, and things have grown well in this dirt before. Garden soil from the ground is too heavy and actually "too dirty" for use in containers; however, it can be a part of a container mix, as will be shown later in this chapter. The rules change when you go from yard gardens to those in containers because the ability for air to reach your plants and their drainage is greatly affected. Ignoring this fact will cause your plants to have poor outcomes, or they may even die.

It is interesting to note that these types of soils do not contain soil at all. They are referred to as soil mixtures, potting soil, container mix, artificial media, and some even include the word soil-less. These mixtures are well aerated, sterile, and lightweight. They contain an excellent balance of organic materials and mineral particles such as peat, sand, and perlite. Since they are soil-less, this means they will not have any dirt in them.

Different manufacturers offer various recipes for container soils. Still, in a nutshell, a good mix will consist of one part vermiculite, one part potting soil, one part compost, and one part sphagnum peat moss. If you don't have compost, you can add a fertilizer that slowly releases nutrients.

Many mixes for containers begin with organic materials. While there are too many to mention here, some of the basic ones include pine bark, compost, husks from coconuts (also known as coir), and peat.

Because drainage and the ability for air to penetrate the soil are two of the biggest factors in your plant's health, many soil mixtures will contain sand, polystyrene, and perlite. These materials are especially helpful for keeping the weight of heavier soil mixes to a minimum.

You can add fertilizers to the soil that are slowly absorbed and are added before you fill up your containers. This makes food readily available for your plants. Additional food can be added if desired from the top, guaranteeing your plants receive a steady supply of nutrients. There are pre-mixed fertilizers you can buy that make this option affordable and easy.

Finally, it is possible to reuse soil year after year, but as a beginner, I would advise you not to. Many of the nutrients will have been depleted by the end of your plant's growing season.

Additionally, soil that has "aged" can be prone to insects, fungus, and diseases. It would be best to invest in a new round of potting mixtures.

However, as you gain experience, you may want to try your hand at reusing your soil. You can revitalize some of your old soil with additional nutrients. This can be done by removing some of the old soil and replacing it with new.

Types of Container Garden Soil

Part of the challenges of growing plants in containers is the fact that soil cannot regenerate or get additional nutrients from the earth. And also, the container plant's roots cannot spread out or grow deeper into the dirt to obtain extra nutrients. Potted plants depend wholly on us to survive. For these reasons, it is vital to opt for the best soil for container gardening. The question is, how do you know which soil to choose and which to avoid? The following tips will answer the question.

There are various soil "formulas" offered by potting soil manufacturers, and they intended to make things easier for you. Some are an excellent choice for growing ornamental plants and flowers, while others are formulated for growing vegetables and other edibles. Products tagged as "general potting soil" at the nursery are purposely made to provide a moist but well-drained quality that is suitable for most plants. Products tagged "cactus & succulents" are sandier soil that drains quicker, offering a perfect atmosphere for the types of plants that flourish in dry conditions.

Soils tagged "moisture control" usually contains a higher of coco coir, peat moss, and other wetting properties. These types of soils are found to prevent under watering and overwatering, but actually, they're suitable for plants that prefer not too much water, for example, annual flowers and vegetables.

Bear in mind that stuff like garden soil, topsoil, and cheap fill dirt isn't suitable to use in containers. Some beginners to gardening do, out of ignorance, use garden dirt in pots. They believe since their plants thrive in the garden, the same soil would also work in the pot. Garden soil is not suitable for the container plant for the following reasons:

1. Garden soil contains loads of potentially nasty substances such as weed seeds, disease organisms, bugs, and other creatures. Putting all of these kinds of stuff inside a pot can cause problems for your plants.

2. Garden soil is too weighty for use in pots and would become compacted in no time. When this occurs, the growth of plants becomes very difficult. So, it is ideal to avoid the garden soil and opt for potting soil to make sure your container plants grow well and healthy.

Best Soil for Outdoor Potted Plants

When choosing soil for container plants, make sure you always read the tag to see whether the soil was intended for a specific purpose. The best option for most outdoor potted plants is of good quality, general soil mix. Preferably, open the bag to inspect the consistency of the potting soil mix before buying it because they are all prepared differently and, manufacturers have different formulas.

Here are what to look for in a quality containers soil mixture:

• The medium should be fluffy and light

• It should hold moisture, and at the same time has good drainage

• It must be porous, so, air and water quickly get to the plant' roots

• There should be no weed seeds sprouting in the sack, or tiny bugs flying around it

• The bark and sand in the mix must not be too much

• It should be moist but not soggy and have a pleasant smell

Best Soil for Large Planters

Consider where you intend to grow your plants before choosing the soil to use for your container crops. Do not worry about the weight of containers that would place on the floor, but be mindful of hanging planters. Compost and soil mixes are heavier but are best to use for container sitting on the floor. So, for pots sitting on the ground, opt for the all-purpose potting mix as they generally have compost.

Best Soil for Hanging Baskets and Planter Boxes

If you plan on growing plants in planter boxes and hanging baskets, you must consider the weight of containers. You can imagine how heavy a pot becomes after it is filled up with dirt and soaked with water. So, what is best for these kinds of planters is a soilless potting mix. Coco coir or peat moss is usually the base ingredients for soilless mixes, and they do not have sand or compost.

Avoid Reusing Soil for Containers

Do not reuse soil in pots for these two reasons:

1. The soil might have been contaminated with bugs and disease spores from the preceding year, and this can harm the new plants.

2. It would be stripped of its nutrients or filled with roots from the grown plants.

For these reasons, you are advised to dump the used container garden soil into the compost bin and begin with new, sterilized soil each year. With this, you will be giving your plant a good start. Nevertheless, if you have very large and deep planter boxes or containers, you do not have to dump all of the soil. I suggest you remove the topsoil about 3 to 5 inches and replace it with fresh soil mix before planting in them.

Making Organic Fertilizer & Compost

<u>Organic Fertilizer</u>

Organic fertilizer is most likely going to do best for container gardening. It can also be inexpensive if you do it yourself. You can add many ingredients to whatever you have as well. Dried manure is the best way to have organic fertilizer, and it's one of the cheaper options. You don't need cow manure for your plants to grow well because chicken manure is also a viable option.

Grass clippings can be added into the different pots and plants as well. It's a cheap way to add a little more nutrient to your plants. The grass will decompose quicker if you put it with a cup of water into a five-gallon bucket; it should only take one to two days before you can use this in your pots. You'll see a difference in the plants after only a week or two. They'll be growing healthier due to the rich nitrogen content. Make sure that when the grass has liquefied that you do not put the pure liquid into the plants, but instead you need to mix it with more water before placing it over your plants.

Seaweed is a little harder to get your hands on, but it is also a great way to add well-needed nutrients into plant soil, but you do have to wait for it to decompose. This can take longer than most people would like to wait. This is also best for outside plants due to the smell that decomposing seaweed and other substances may put out. Dried seaweed can also be used to make various organic fertilizers. You can also liquefy the seaweed as you would grass, and after diluting the liquefied form with water, it is a great mixture for organic fertilizer. Seaweed serves as a source of food for soil microbes.

Coffee grounds are great to add in as topsoil to create organic fertilizer. The nitrogen in it will get down into the roots and give the plant a jolt. It's best for fruits like berries, but it also works on my flower plants as well. Just make sure to spread the coffee grounds over the soil before you water, and it'll filter deeper in as the plant is watered. You can do this with used coffee grounds as well, but fresh will pack more of a punch.

Human urine is also great for plants and can be mixed into any fertilizer, homemade or otherwise. It's high in both phosphorus and potassium, which is great for your plants. You'll find these very ingredients in many of the fertilizers that are sold in stores. You need about one cup of urine for every eight cups of water, so make sure that you don't overuse the urine. If you put too much urine in the mixture, it can be detrimental to your plants, just like overwatering.

No matter what you use in your human fertilizer, you need to make sure that it's a mixture. You can add these together, but don't forget to dilute all the substances so that you don't over-fertilize your plants. Container gardening is all about using what's right for the plants you're growing. Usually, you'll be growing small to medium-sized plants that don't require a lot of attention or fertilizer, so make sure that you're careful with the amounts you provide.

Compost:

If you'd like to get a barrel with a lid, or other containers similar, it's easy to make your compost as well. In the container, you'd put various pieces of fruits and vegetables to decompose. The smaller the pieces that are put into the container means the faster the decomposition. This will produce a fertilizer that is both organic and packs a punch that will make your container garden thrive and produce beautifully. It's best to use this type of fertilizer with fruits and vegetables to add flavor.

It's also a great idea to mix in eggshells. Crushing the eggshells before you put them in will help them to decompose faster. The food will smell as it's rotting, so it's recommended that all composts are kept outside. When covered, the smell will decrease, but so will the rate of decomposition, eggshells are very high on calcium carbonate, which is the same thing found in lime, and it's great to fend off blossom end rot. It also makes your fruit grow better.

If you put potato ends into the compost, you have to be careful that potatoes don't start growing in the soil. It'll eat up the nutrients from your composition, but you would have very healthy and ready to eat potatoes that are packed with flavor. This is the same for any root related plant.

However, the best thing to do for roses and most other flowers as well as banana peels. These decompose easily, and they'll keep your flowers very vibrant. Though they can also just be thrown in at the bottom of the dirt you use for planting, and then they'll decompose naturally without smell, but adding them into the mixture will help make your organic fertilizer that much better.

CHAPTER 6:

The Best Vegetables for Containers

Vegetables Right from the Pot

<u>Tomatoes</u>

Tomatoes tend to be one of the vegetables people grow in containers when they first start gardening. Here are a few important things to know about tomatoes:

1. If you decide to grow them, plant them in a large container that is at least fourteen inches in diameter. Additionally, when larger pots are used, tomato plants often respond by getting bigger and producing more fruit.

2. When buying soil for your containers, make sure they are labeled appropriately for larger pots. These will contain ingredients like perlite.com.posted pine bark, peat moss, rice hulls, coconut pieces, and peanut shells to give your soil some bulk. Avoid mixtures that are high in peat moss

because these will cause compression of your soil, thus causing the plant's root mass to be reduced.

3. You will need a vertical support system, like a small trellis. This should be installed around your tomato plant soon after planting, so you do not damage your plant as it grows.

4. Never overwater your tomatoes, and be sure to keep the soil moist instead of wet. You could use self-watering containers to make sure that the plant gets the water it needs.

5. You will want to feed your plants with a slow-release fertilizer and provide it with at least six to eight hours of sunlight every day. It is best to plant tomatoes in the late spring as this lessens their chances of being damaged from frosts.

6. Harvesting tomatoes when they are red means they have reached maturity and are ready to be enjoyed.

Peppers

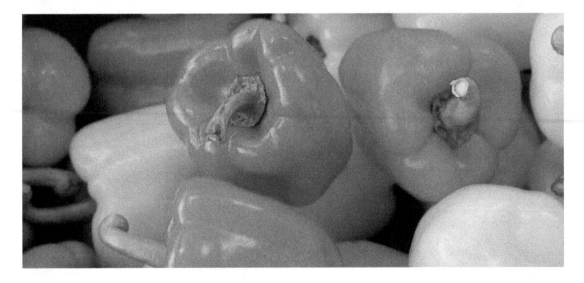

If you decide to grow peppers, which are also quite popular, strive to find varieties that are labeled, "intended for containers" or "compact." This means these varieties tend not to grow as big as regular varieties meant for in-ground gardens. Here are some helpful facts to know about peppers:

1. Peppers don't require too much space to grow. You can grow them in containers starting at nine inches in diameter and about nine inches deep.

2. You will want to buy soil that is labeled for larger containers because this includes bulk materials like pine bark, peanut shells, and other hulls, which will help keep the soil from becoming too dense. Also, make sure the soil remains moist, even when its surface becomes dried out.

3. Be sure to supply trellis support for your peppers, so when they become tall, they will not become damaged by falling over.

4. You can feed it with fertilizer once every week and cover the soil with mulch so it will retain moisture.

5. Sunlight exposure should be direct in the morning and filtered all day long as the afternoon sun can burn the crop.

6. Peppers are usually grown during early spring.

7. The peppers are ready to pick when their color and size have reached maturity.

Beans

Beans are another vegetable easily grown in containers. Beans are tasty, easy to grow, and they freeze well, too. Here are a few recommendations if you decide to grow your own:

1. You will need a container about twelve inches wide. If you are growing bush beans, the container depth should be six to seven inches, whereas pole beans require a depth closer to eight or nine inches.

2. With several varieties, you will need to provide a trellis for the plant to grow up on to support the weight of the plant.

3. Consider using pasteurized soil (soil that has been baked in the oven), mix it with compost, and add mulch to help retain the soil's moisture.

4. Make sure you place your containers in a warm or brightly lit location but avoid direct sunlight.

5. You may need to water the beans frequently to keep the soil moist, too.

6. You can plant your seedlings in the spring once the soil has warmed up.

7. When the pods are fully elongated and are crisp and firm, it is time to harvest them. When they reach maturity, be sure to harvest them every day. Frequent harvesting will encourage more beans to be produced from your plant.

Squash/Zucchini

Squash and zucchini fall into the cucurbit category of plants (as do cucumbers). These may not be vegetables you think of right away for growing, but they are not difficult to do and are delicious straight from the garden—raw or cooked. Here are several guidelines to be aware of:

1. Cucurbit plants can be grown in any container that is twelve inches in diameter. Two plants are easily grown side by side in a fourteen-inch-diameter container.

2. Choose a good quality potting so il and mix it with organic matter before planting your seedlings.

3. Make sure your plants get at least eight hours of sunlight per day and be sure to water them often. Do more watering if your container is made of clay rather than plastic because this type of container can cause the soil to dry out faster.

4. Begin to fertilize your plants with a timed-release formula after the first real leaves begin to appear.

5. Plant your seedlings in early to mid-summer. This variety of plants are very easy to start from seeds, taking about three to four weeks before it is time to transplant into containers. However, many like me just plant the seeds directly into the containers.

6. Depending upon the varieties you choose, cucurbits begin to ripen after 45 days. Consider starting new plants four to six weeks after your initial planting to produce fresh throughout the summer.

7. Winter squashes will be ready to harvest about 100 days after planting. If you planted summer squashes, you can pick them when the fruits become about eight inches long and three inches in diameter.

Cucumbers

Because cucumbers are in the cucurbit family, much of what I stated above applies here as well.

1. You need to use a large container that has a diameter of at least 12 inches.

2. Cucumbers need loose soil that reaches 70 degrees Fahrenheit and has good drainage.

3. They also need organic fertilizer to sustain their nutritional needs.

4. Cucumbers are plants that need eight hours of direct exposure to sunlight.

5. Harvest your cucumbers when they are about seven to nine inches long.

Beets

Beets are great container plants as long as you have them in a pot that's twelve inches deep. You can grow up to six regular-sized beets in one pot, and even more of the smaller, baby variety in the same pot.

Carrots

One of the most 'easy to grow' vegetables and also commonly consumed one. They manage to live well in containers too. Since growing carrots is an effortless process, a good choice for beginners. It may not save a considerable amount of yours, but growing carrots at home ensure you of quality and a healthy supply of vegetables.

If you're interested in growing carrots in a container pot, then you might want to start with these varieties.

• Short n Sweet

• Thumbelina

• Little Fingers

They're all baby carrot varieties that shouldn't get longer than four to five inches, but in case they do, have a pot that's at least twelve inches deep, if not more.

Cole Crop

These are broccoli, cauliflower, and cabbage, and they are some of the easiest vegetables to grow in a container garden. You should not plant a lot of types in a single pot because they won't be able to grow. Give each plant a pot for enough space.

Cucumber

If you want to grow cucumbers in containers, then you might want to try the Bush Pickle or Salad Bush varieties. The plants are going to come out of the edges of the pot and may need a little trellis to keep them upright, so be prepared for maintenance with cucumbers.

One of the most 'simple to grow' item in the list, cucumbers can grow well in containers. You can get a large yield with minimum efforts. Though they grow well in pots, they do not grow well in winter. So, wait until the end of the winter season and then begin plantation.

Eggplant

Eggplants only need pots that are twelve inches wide by five inches deep, but they are going to need some staking to keep them upright.

Lettuce and Micro Greens

If you want to start easy, then grow some lettuce and microgreens. The size of the pot doesn't come into play with these. Just take a little fertile soil, some seeds, and keep the soil moist so that you get some homegrown salad greens!

To have lettuces on your catalog of container vegetable gardening is perhaps a wise thing. The quality yield of it will turn out to be a profitable affair, and you will be satisfied to get a good return for your efforts (though you may not need to put more because lettuces are simple to grow at home). They love to be alone, so do not plant lettuces with full of other vegetables around. Give the attention it deserves, checks that the soil is not wet, protect it from strong sun rays, and again don't forget to keep adding a moderate amount of slow-releasing fertilizers, preferably compost but don't overfeed.

Melons

If you've ever heard of the dwarf melons like Bush Sugar Baby, then you've heard of a plant that seems to have been made specifically for container gardening. These are micro watermelon types that will need a little support when they begin to get fruit, or they could rip out of the pot.

Onions

Green onions are the best for growing in containers. All you need is a bag of sets, a pot around four to five inches deep, and some loose soil. You can grow onions until they are their regular size.

This one has largely consumed items a cross-world. Again 'easy to grow' one, perhaps it could top the list of vegetables that can be grown effortlessly. Needs no special attention. Just sow the seeds of it and leave it on its fate, except adding some fertilizers and watering them regularly.

Peas

If you're planting the baby pea varieties, you can plant six plants in a twelve-inch deep pot. The baby pea varieties are:

• Maestro

• Green Arrow

• Sugar Bon Snap Pea

• English Peas

Potatoes

Second, in the rank of best-suited vegetable for container gardening. Again, for some reason that it is a widely consumed item, potatoes make a good choice. Do not plant it with tomatoes. Potatoes need little large and deep containers.

It's great to grow your potatoes, and they're easy to grow in pots! You just need a twelve-inch pot for three to four potatoes. Keep giving it water, so the plants produce and make sure the stems are covered fully with the soil. In a few months, you'll get some early potatoes. If you have patience, you'll have even larger ones!

Turnips

Since turnips do not require sunlight all the time, it is a fine option to consider for indoor vegetable plantation or to be put in shady areas in garden. Some varieties of turnips are ripe within as soon as one month, so it should be considered for interim plantation.

Parsley

Being high on demand, parsley is the fine choice to have it in the garden. This herb manages well in containers, and you may find them planted in window boxes and pots when it comes to container gardening. Little more care needs to be taken. No ordinary soil and addition of some fertile supplements can do the magic.

Cabbage

Here the list comes to the fine selection for salad. Widely consumed and cherished vegetables across borders, cabbage is high nutrient requiring vegetable and needs little more care. Consider companion planting if you have cabbage on your list of vegetables for container gardening. It needs a good bed, some slow-release fertilizers, and shady space to help it grow well.

Sweet Corn

Yet another most preferred item in container vegetable gardening, because the name itself denotes that it tastes too good. Nutritional item, so you should include it in your diet itinerary.

Being a deep-rooted vegetable, sweet corn needs a deep container, and since it grows high, it necessarily has to be out under the sky. It requires relatively low nutrients, so a good option to post-harvest replacement of high nutrient demanding plants.

Hops

Hops keep growing until they are well fed. If you love homemade wine and wish to do it yourself, growing hops are just the perfect choice to plant in containers. These growing hops value your hard work and return you the desired yield for longer times.

Lettuces

Lettuces fall into four different categories: Loose Leaf, Romaine (also known as Cos), Butterheads, and Crisphead. While each has its own characteristics, there are some similarities between them:

1. It is best to plant lettuce seeds directly into a six-to twelve-inch-diameter container that you want them to grow in. They do not transplant well. They only take about one week to germinate and make sure your plants are eight to ten inches apart.

2. Lettuces tend to grow best in cooler temperatures.

3. Use a standard soil mix formulated to provide nutrients and one that will hold moisture. You can mix the soil with compost to make it even healthier.

4. These vegetables grow very successfully in containers, enabling you to keep pests, snails, and slugs under control.

5. Do not place these vegetables in direct sunlight. Instead, place them in a shady place for the best results.

6. Lettuces need to be harvested within a week of when they are ready, or the leaves will begin to bolt. When this happens, a flower stalk will appear, will go to seed, and the leaves become bitter tasting. Therefore, plant only the amount you plan to use.

7. The plant itself grows quickly, especially when soil conditions are healthy.

8. Be sure your containers drain well but also make sure the soil remains moist.

9. Lettuce plants require little to no fertilizer if you are using good soil.

10. Lettuces will be ready to harvest anywhere from eight to fourteen weeks.

11. The best method for enjoying lettuce throughout the growing season is to plan to sow a few lettuces seeds every two weeks. Then, when you harvest the lettuce, be sure to put up the whole plant. This will discourage diseases in the ground and rotting.

Choosing your Vegetables

Naturally, you will want to choose vegetables that do not take up a lot of space for them to grow. Most vegetables will grow well together in a single container, and it is up to your creativity on how to mix and match the different vegetables together.

Tomatoes, peppers, and eggplant are ideal container garden vegetables if your space gets at least 6 hours of direct sunlight. Choose varieties such as Tumbler or Sweet Million tomatoes to grow them in limited space easily.

Carrots and radishes are also great root crops for a container garden. See if your local garden center has available globe or round radish and carrot varieties that can thrive in troughs or boxes.

Potatoes can also be grown in large pots or buckets and will produce a lot of spuds. You will start by planting the tubers and filling up the top space with more compost as it continues to grow.

Beans and peas are other great choices for a container garden. Opt for the dwarf varieties which can grow well in containers. You can create wigwams on top of the containers to allow them to grow and thrive in the limited amount of space available.

Mushrooms can be grown at any time of the year indoors. You will need a special compost that contains mushroom spawn. It will need to be placed in a dark and draft-free area of around 50 to 60 degrees F (or 10 to 15 degrees C) and should be watered regularly. You can also choose to create your organic compost using straw and then buy an activator to grow your mushrooms.

Ultimately, you should choose to plant the vegetables that you and your family like to eat. Grow local vegetables in your area that give a lot of produce despite the limitations in space.

CHAPTER 7:

How to Plant Vegetables in containers

You've prepared your soil, taken care to choose your seeds and seedlings, and now you feel ready to dig in, literally, and begin planting. Before you let any tool dig into that soil, you may be interested in learning a few secrets. Others have learned about growing plants from seeds. While it's not difficult, there is a certain knack to it.

Too often, well-meaning novice gardeners plow on based solely on intuition or worse yet on bad advice from others.

You may have already talked to fellow gardeners who couldn't resist relating their own horror stories about starting plants from seeds. These stories are something akin to urban legends for gardeners.

Start with good soil, and half the "battle" is already won. If you're going to scrimp and save, don't do it on your growing medium. Buy what's known as a sterile seed-starting mix. If you have trouble finding it, ask your local nursery staff about it. This mix contains more nutrients than regular soil. And your germinating seeds can use this.

This mix is also lighter than other soils. Some of these mixes even include fertilizer as well as wetting agents. It is well worth the extra expense.

Not only is your soil important, but the containers you place these seeds in are vital as well. If you're planning on reusing pots or cell packs, then take some precautions. The best precaution you can take is the sterilization of the cell packs.

To sterilize these containers, you first wash them well in warm soapy water. Then you rinse the packs in a mixture of water and bleach. And then you rinse the rinse. You put the packs through a second rinse to remove any bleach residue. Once you allow the containers to air dry, then you can begin to plant.

Roll Out that Seedling Mat

Have you ever heard of a seedling mat? It's a heated mat specifically used to help small starter plants grow. You can use this same mat under your cell packs to aid in the germination process. Your seeds will sprout faster, and their roots will grow healthier. Just be sure to set the mat at the proper temperature for the types of seeds you're growing. This information should be on the seed packet.

For best results, don't try using old seeds. Not even in last years. Buy fresh seeds, and you'll help to guarantee your greatest success. If you're not sure whether the seeds you have on hand are fresh, simply put them in a glass of water. If they sink, the seed is fresh. If it floats, it's old, and chances are good it won't sprout. Once you've determined the fresh seeds, simply dry them off and plant them. It doesn't get much easier than that.

Seeds Need Drainage

Your newly planted seeds require good drainage. The biggest mistake many novice gardeners make is to overwater them. Give these small things too much moisture, and you're exposing them to the possibility of getting a fungal infection. This infection is sometimes referred to as "damping-off." More often than not, it's caused by a combination of overwatering and a lack of proper air circulation.

Some horticulturists recommend that you cover the seeds with of mix of milled sphagnum and starter chicken grit – which is nothing more than finely ground stone. This keeps the soil dry while providing an inhospitable environment. To ensure good air circulation, many gardeners have fans blowing on the seeds. If you want to try this, keep the fan pointed low. You aim to have it blow across the containers. This is the area where the air is more likely to get trapped and get stagnant.

Transplanting Your New Plants

Once your seeds have started to sprout, they'll need to be transplanted. Your first instinct is to empty your cell packs of your newly grown seedlings and plant them outside if that's their final destination. Before you expose them full time to the permanent home, you need to introduce them to the direct sunlight gently. This is vital for all seeds, but especially important if you're transplanting herb seedlings.

Acclimating small plants to the sun is referred to as hardening off. While the seedlings are still in their original containers, place the seedlings in a shaded area, so they only receive indirect sunlight for a few hours during the day. If you have a porch or patio that's facing north, this is the ideal place for them. After a few days, you can leave them outside overnight, as long as you bring them in when the weather is expected to dip below freezing. If the seeds are slated to be planted in the shade, then after several days of this indirect sunlight, you can then transplant them into your garden.

If they're plants that require direct sunlight, they need to be gently exposed to direct sunlight. But do this slowly. Start with one hour of the sun for the first day and slowly increase the hours of exposure to the sun daily. Do this for about a week. After that, you should be able to place them in the garden without fear.

Believe it or not, your seedlings will go into shock when they're transplanted as they get accustomed to their new environment. For this reason, you'll want to choose the late afternoon on a cloudy day actually to place them in their new home. If the weather refuses to cooperate with you and you can't get a nice cloudy day, then do the following best thing: wait until dusk, when the sun is only beginning to set. This helps them avoid the harsh sun and provide them with a better recovery period. Don't become alarmed when you see your small plants droop and wilt some. This is perfectly normal. They'll soon perk up.

Skip the "Middleman": Planting Seeds Directly into The Ground

Some plants grow better when the seeds are sown directly into the garden skipping the "middleman" as it were of the indoor germination process. Seeds especially suited to this are usually the large ones and sprout plants that grow rather fast. You may want to start the following seeds right in your garden: corn, peas, beans, melons, and squash. Of course, this is merely a partial list.

As with everything else in gardening, you'll want to be fully prepared before you sow the seeds. Ensure the soil is dry enough for planting as well as warm enough. Yes, warm enough! If the soil is too cold, then there's a possibility that the seeds will rot before they have a chance to germinate. Peas, for example, love the cooler soil. You can plant these in the soil as cool as 40 degrees.

On the other hand, you're considering including squash in your garden; then your soil needs to be warmer, some fifteen degrees or so. Squash seeds germinate best when the dirt is approximately 65 degrees.

So how can you tell the temperature of your soil? You guessed it – with a soil thermometer. And yes, there is such a thing and you can easily find one of these at your local nursery.

Once you've planted the seeds, be patient. Once they show their true leaves, which are the second set, which breaks through the dirt, you can then transplant them. Without a doubt, you'll need to move some out of their original home to thin them out. This provides them with the room they'll eventually need as they grow.

If you transplant these seedlings, you'll find that, just like the seedlings you've transplant from indoors to their outdoor home, they may go into shock. They may wilt some. But again, don't worry, they'll perk up soon enough.

Tips on How to Reduce Container Gardening Costs

Assess why you are into container gardening. It is the foundation of your garden. If your motive is to earn, then you can plan the plants that you are going to have, the materials that you would need, and other pertinent data. However, if you have no solid reasons why you are into this, you would just do things without regard to the future, and you might spend unnecessarily. If you have finally decided why you are bent on having container gardening, then you can do smart planning.

Write down your plans. You would see the overall picture when you write down your thoughts, strategies, ideas, and blueprint of your garden. You would also be able to list down all the things you would need when you have a picture of your plans and not just a mental image. Plus, you could estimate the timeframe you need to complete your garden.

Make a to-buy list ahead of time and keep an eye on the costs. You can check how much you would need when you plan your garden needs. You could do your shopping at the end of the season sales and save money. Buy the items and supplies that you need throughout the year and store them until they are required. When you do not know the things you need for the whole year, you tend to buy them according to the time you need them, and that could be costly for you.

Study how you would go about your plans. You can ask the opinions of other garden experts or enthusiasts or ask for help from friends or other people you know who are into container gardening. You could adjust your plans when you acquire better suggestions or ideas.

Thorough planning would save you money and cause you to spend less than necessary for your container gardening.

Tips to lessen your container gardening expenses

Start from seeds

Most seeds cost less than a dollar. If you would start from scratch, it may take some time and more effort, but you would save a lot. As you go looking for seeds for your container garden, you might find be confused with some of the terms used for describing seeds. For your clarification:

F1 varieties or hybrids

It is the expensive seeds as the process of producing these seeds is more complicated than usual. The crossing of two-parent varieties is done so that a new one will be created.

Genetically modified

These seeds are created in the laboratories where their genes are manipulated.

Open-pollinated varieties

Also known as heirloom varieties, these seeds can be reused year after year. They are found to be more resistant to various crop diseases.

Organic seed

Grown without the use of pesticides, fungicides, herbicides, or fertilizers.

For newbies, choose the "easy seeds" to plant. These are hardy and easy to plant, plus they grow earlier, too.

Buy seedlings

Having healthy, young plants also cost less in the long run. They have a higher probability of surviving than seeds. Lesser efforts are required to ensure that they survive the transfer to another occasion. When buying seedlings, make sure to check the leaves; they should be green, and if there are patches of white or dried leaves, avoid these plants as they could mean weak or unhealthy plants. They may not last long when you transplant them. Check also if they are firmly attached to a group. Trying to separate and plant them could cause trauma to the plant and cause its death. Those planted singly are easier to transplant and have a higher probability of surviving a transplant. Also, do not just depend on the height of the plants to determine if they can survive. It has been noticed that smaller plants do better at staying alive when transplanted.

Buy all your garden needs during the sale.

It usually takes place every end of the growing season. At this time, containers are marked down at half prices. Even other supplies such as tools and decorative supplies would cost less. Therefore, if you have any garden need that can wait until the clearance sales, acquire them during that time and save money.

Propagate your seedlings.

Some seedlings are effortless to propagate. Instead of buying many of these plants, just be the one to multiply them and save money. Look for plants that can be spread only by simply cutting branches and putting them in water. When roots start to come from those branches, plant them in containers or pots. There is even something better than this. Some plants just propagate on-their-own. All you have to do is to transplant them when they are strong enough to be transferred to a different container from the mother plant.

Recycle

Instead of buying containers, take a closer look at things in your house. Maybe there are old pails that you can use as pots. Old baskets can be redecorated and be used as vases in your container gardening. Be creative and imaginative and transform those old buckets or bottles into something useful. You would discover that there are many things in your house (specifically in your attic or basement) that can be recycled and converted into garden items.

Exchange seeds or seedlings with others.

Instead of looking and buying seeds and seedlings from garden centers, contact friends who are garden container enthusiasts and strike a deal with them. You can trade seeds and seedlings. You would not have to spend money at all, plus that is also building camaraderie with other gardeners.

Make your compost.

Instead of buying fertilizers, you can make your compost in your backyard. Simply dig a small portion, and leftovers and other biodegradable things can be placed there. Not only have you saved money for fertilizer or compost, but you have also helped the environment by cutting the garbage being sent to landfills.

Compare and contrast prices.

You can save money when you try to check different stores, flea markets, yard sales, and thrift stores. Sometimes, one tends to patronize a specific store, and he or she misses other great deals at different stores. You can also check online for the most significant sales and best offers of different shops. Look for coupons or vouchers too in your daily newspapers.

Choose edible plants.

Instead of buying exotic and expensive plants, be practical, and buy things that you could use in your kitchen. You do not only save money on caring for those strange plants, but you also save grocery money when you harvest your vegetables or herbs in your container garden. Think of all the herbs and vegetables that you always need in your kitchen like garlic, ginger, parsley or celery and plant them. Whenever you need any of these, you do not have to shell out cash. Just go to your garden and harvest from them. Plus, this might motivate you to start a little business and increase your income all the more. Neighbors or friends could just order some of your products instead of buying them in the local grocery stores. You could also try edible flowers. That way, you have house décor and ingredients for dishes at the same time.

Place an ad, use your social media accounts or the word of mouth advertisement, and just inform other people that you are into container gardening.

You would be amazed at how sometimes people just offer many tips, items or even plants for you, for free. For some people, instead of having tools or gardening supplies that are not being used in their homes or just adding spaces in their garage or sheds, they would instead give them to other garden enthusiasts if they know they require those. You save money, and at the same time, you have helped those people dispose of the items they consider as junk in their homes.

One does not need to spend so much. Be wise and use these tips and see how much you can save by doing so.

CHAPTER 8:

Plant Combinations and Companion Planting

Companion Planting

The idea of companion planting has been providing excellent results to the container farmers. It involves the planting combinations of specific plants for the mutual benefits of the plants involved. The concept here is that individual plants do help each other in taking up nutrients and helping with the management of pests, while also attracting pollinators. Nevertheless, research is still on the way to find out more planting combination that works fine. There are a few that are listed here that have been scientifically proven and will also work fine in your container garden.

Melons or Squash with Flowering Herbs

All the vegetables here are known to need pollinators for production. Therefore, you can plant flowering herbs such as fennel, parsley, and dill close to the squash or melon to invite insect visitors into your garden. The only way to get enough yields of these vegetables is through pollination.

Calendula with Broccoli

Calendula flowers are known to produce a sticky substance from their stems, which in turn attracts aphids and gets them trapped there. Planting them beside the brassica crops such as the broccoli will help to deter aphids from broccoli while also attracting beneficial ladybugs to dine on the aphids.

Radishes with Carrots

Both radishes and carrots take up nutrients from different locations in the soil, so they do not compete for nutrients or other resources. Their fast growth characterizes radishes, and they do not grow as deeply as carrots do. Carrots generally have long taproots, and it takes more time for them to mature when compared to Radishes.

Lettuce with Tomatoes or Eggplants

These plants are characterized by different growth habits, which makes them beneficial to each other. Tomatoes and eggplants will generally grow taller; thereby, they are useful in shading cool-season crops like lettuce that doesn't like heat at all. Growing them with tomatoes or eggplants will also help in extending their harvest period.

Nasturtium with Cucumber

This combination involves introducing both pollinators and beneficial insects into your garden, which will, in turn, help in improving biodiversity. Nasturtiums are characterized by a unique scent that helps in repelling pests and also growing in a colorful tumble underneath.

Tomatoes with Basil or Cilantro

Apart from the belief that planting basil alongside tomatoes helps to improve the flavor of tomatoes, basil also has a strong scent that helps to prevent pests. As an added advantage, when basil or cilantro is allowed to spout flower, it will result in bringing in the pollinators.

Corn, Pole beans with Squash or Pumpkin

These combinations are popularly referred to as the three sisters. Corn gives pole beans a platform for climbing, while beans will convert atmospheric oxygen into a form that can be used by both plants. Squash and pumpkin are leaves spreading plants, thereby creating living mulch that helps in reducing weeds as well as holding of moisture.

Lettuce with Chives or Garlic

Planting of chives or garlic, which is characterized by strong smell will help in repelling aphids, thus protecting your Lettuce. You can also add alyssum nearby to help invite beneficial insects.

Sweet Alyssum with Swiss chard

Alyssum is an annual crop that can be quickly grown from seed between the rows of vegetables, and it is known to attract hoverflies. The Hoverflies are beneficial insects that help in the control of aphids.

Chamomile with Cabbage

Chamomile helps in inviting beneficial insects for a variety of brassicas such as cabbage. You can cut off the Chamomile and leave to get decomposed on the bed while allowing the roots to remain intact to decay and help add nutrients to the soil.

Roses with Geraniums or Chives

Generally, plants that exhibit strong smell or taste will help in deterring aphids and beetle. Though it has not been entirely proven that this works, it worth trying to prevent roses from being eaten by beetle or aphids that multiply rapidly.

Bad Companion

Corn:

Avoid planting corn and tomatoes together, as they both attract the same tomato fruit-worm.

Cucumber:

Sage should be avoided near cucumber, as it is generally harmful to the cucumber plant.

Kohlrabi

Do not grow alongside pole beans, peppers, strawberry, or tomatoes.

Lettuce

Does not prosper well beside cabbage, as the cabbage stunts growth and reduces the flavor of lettuce.

Leeks

Avoid planting leeks near legumes. (peas, beans, peanuts or alfalfa).

Parsnip

Grows well alongside bush bean, onion, garlic, pepper, potato, and squash.

Peas:

Onions and garlic stunt the growth of peas.

Potatoes:

Tomatoes and potatoes should not be planted together as they attract the same blight.

Radish:

Avoid planting hyssop near radishes.

With that in mind, and notwithstanding the above list, here is a selection of popular vegetables and their particular needs, that can be grown in your KG.

This list includes instructions for growing these vegetables in a traditional 'row' garden, but this is easily adapted with the KG garden in mind.

CHAPTER 9:

Providing the Right growing condition

Nearly Weed-Free Gardening

Weeds are not only unsightly, but they also rob your plants of much-needed nutrients. But weeds are also an unavoidable fact of life. You'll never be able to eliminate weeds even for the small space completely you're using. The best you can do is control them. To that end, there is an easy way to make the "weed-control patrol" easier and less intense.

First, you start "clean" each growing season. Save all the newspapers and cardboard you can throughout the winter. When spring arrives, you then cover your garden beds with it. You'll want to layer these materials, so they're about an inch and a half thick.

By doing this, you're effectively outsmarting the weeds. Keeping the seeds warm triggers germination. The seeds, though, aren't receiving any sunlight, so they die relatively quickly.

Don't remove the covering when you start planting. Simply create a hole through this layer of material, which by now should be mostly decomposed. To ensure that no seeds of unwanted plants are spread throughout the spring, you'll want to take an extra precautionary measure. Place yet another layer of newspapers around your growing plants.

Regardless of how you're controlling your weeds, you still need to check your garden daily to ensure they aren't overtaking your plot. Many gardeners choose either the early morning hours or the early evening to weed. But, if you want to increase the odds those unwanted guests don't return, you should weed during the heat of the day. This stresses them out. Unfortunately, this is the time it may very well stress you out as well! It's also best to weed after a good rain or a thorough watering session. The wet soil is looser, and the weeds are easier to pull.

Feeding your plants

When it comes to feeding your vegetable planters, then the debate goes on as to whether or not to go organic and dump the chemical fertilizers altogether.

Feeding organically, with the use of well-rotted manure, for instance, takes a bit more preparation than just throwing a handful of 'growmore' at your vegetables. However, I believe the results are worth the effort.

Well prepared compost should include where possible, a mix of well-rotted manure or composted material from your kitchen, for instance. Mix this through with your 'store-bought' compost if you have none of your own. This will ensure that your vegetables get a good start.

If you are using your compost from your composting bin, be sure to take the compost from the bottom of the pile. This is 'the good stuff' and should be crumbly and not wet or smelly. This would indicate the compost was not ready for planting.

What you are doing is adding a balanced diet. N(Nitrogen), .P(Potassium), and .K (Phosphorus) – the key ingredients to a happy plant!

If you are using chemical fertilizer, then you should look out for this designation on the box, where N.P.K is usually marked according to the mix.

Nitrogen loving vegetables like cabbage or spinach, for instance, like a higher percentage of .N in the mix, whereas peas and beans get their nitrogen from the air and so do not need strong nitrogen-based formula.

Most marketers of chemical fertilizers nowadays have this marked on the box, even designating the vegetable types that the fertilizer is best for.

Fruiting plants like tomatoes need plenty of potassium and calcium, especially when bearing fruit to maintain a healthy crop.

Watering your planters

Water enables the nutrients in the soil to energize the plant through the roots.

The process of photosynthesis means the plant uses light, carbon dioxide, and water to make sugar.

As mentioned, planters are indeed prone to either drying out to quickly or getting waterlogged by overwatering. Whether by nature or nurture-so to speak. Water logging blocks the oxygen source to the roots of the plant, and so the plant dies unless remedial action is taken in time.

Fungal diseases also thrive in wet conditions, making this a "double whammy" for the poor plant.

How do you know if your plants are overwatered? Well the tell-tale signs that a plant is getting too much water are:

- Leaves yellowing from the bottom up

- Soil turning green

- Grey mold appears on the plant

- The plant has stopped growing

- The plant is wilting badly

Prevention of this is simple. Make sure that you have prepared your planter properly as per the earlier instructions. Do not be too enthusiastic when it comes to watering, but even if you are, proper drainage should allow for the soil to reach a natural level.

Be observant! just watch your plants for the signs of overwatering and be ready to remedy the situation. If there is indeed fungal growth, then you may have to apply a fungicide to remedy it.

Signs of under watering include.

- Dry, hard soil or compost

- Plant leaves tend to go brown and crisp

- Plant shrivels and dies!

Will you notice the list here is shorter? The fact is that many more plants die from overwatering than the opposite, largely because the overwatering starves the roots of oxygen and so the plant reacts faster in many cases.

Mulching

I am a keen advocate of mulching in general, for the reasons listed below.

1. Mulching keeps in the moisture content around the plant where it is most needed.

2. It suppresses weeds that would otherwise fight your plants for nutrients and water.

3. As the mulch rots, it adds nutrients and humus into the soil, improving the soil condition and crop yield.

4. Though not mulch – if you cover the soil with a weed suppressant fabric, this will also warm the soil slightly – good for early growth.

These attributes apply to vegetables grown in containers as well as in traditional vegetable beds.

Bark chippings are my favorite mulching material for my pathways between the vegetable beds, or indeed the planters I have around a particular area.

This is easy to walk on and prevents mud from being spread around in the wetter weather, as well as acting as an excellent weed-suppressor.

For cucumbers, marrows, strawberries, etc., I use just straw to mulch. This gives the vegetables a dry bed and discourages the dreaded slug.

That said, if you have a lawn that needs constant mowing (as they do), then the good idea is to use the lawn clippings as a mulch. Spread this about 2-3 inches thick between the veggies and allow them to rot down to produce a nitrogen-rich feed for the plants.

For a more effective weed-suppressant, lay out some newspaper or cardboard before adding the lawn clippings.

However, it has to be said that unlike planting in a garden or perhaps a raised bed, growing vegetables in planters usually means that there is not much space for mulching. However, it is still worth-while, and perhaps more relevant when your planters are prone to dry out quickly.

Sunlight

Most people wildly overestimate the amount of sun their container is going to get. While you can find good plants for almost any type of light, you have to know how much light the container is going to get before you choose a plant. To figure out how much light the container is going to get, set it where it's going to be placed and time when the light hits it, and when the light is no longer hitting it. You can also purchase a sun calculator in order to do this for you. Without enough sunlight, some plants are going to shrivel and die. They'll slowly fade away into nothing and you won't know what's happening to them. With too much light, some plants are going to wilt and burn, so they're equally as unhealthy. So always be sure you have the proper amount of light!

Container tomatoes need at least 6 to 8 hours of sunlight a day in order for them to produce fruit well and have a good harvest. Balconies and porches are great places to achieve this, but if you choose to grow them indoors, they must be in a place where they can get maximum sunlight, even if it means moving it from window to window. Take note, however, that too much heat can be harmful to tomatoes. Containers can heat up quickly in the summertime, especially if the container is dark-colored. When this happens, the root of the plants will be too hot for them to be able to set tomatoes. They will still blossom, but the flowers will just fall off.

Staking

It is needed to stake or support plants such as tomatoes. Do not wait long before staking potted tomatoes. An ideal is to place 2 to 3 stakes or cages because bush varieties will need them to help in supporting their branches and heavy fruit sets. Add the stakes or cages when planting the container. Staking is optional but is recommended.

Pruning

Pruned tomato plants will produce less fruit, but they will be larger. There are two methods used in pruning tomato plants, and each has its own advantages. The first method is pruning the plant by pinching away the suckers, which are the shoots that grow between the stem and the leaf stalk and do not contain blossoms. If you decide to go with this method, it should be done once a week to keep the plant free of the suckers.

The second way of pruning is by not actually pruning them and just to let the plant grow wild. Plants that are not pruned will require less water and produce more fruit, the downside being that the fruit will be smaller, and the plant would need greater space to grow.

Managing Disease and Pests

<u>T. Fuller</u>

The life of a gardener would be much simpler if gardeners were the only ones who liked to eat vegetables. But many other creatures, large, small, and very small, like to eat the fruits of their labor. Regardless of their size or shape, garden pests are every gardener's nightmare. The good news is from the start: container gardeners are unlikely to mind the pest problems most country gardeners have in their gardens. A potted garden on a balcony or porch, or even a paved part, probably has no pests because they are smart enough not to waste time on food in places they have never had. Many plant diseases that occasionally affect ground gardeners, for example, Verticillium wilt, live on the garden soil. The garden soils on the containers do not have garden soil; therefore, they are also free of diseases living in the soil. Other diseases, such as flower top rot, are caused by uneven watering, which will not be a problem if you use automatic watering cans. Good compost, which makes up about half of the soil in the container I use, can help prevent all kinds of plant diseases.

Thief Gallery

"Something" eats small holes in the leaves of my cabbages. "Something" ate everything but the stem of a bean seedling last night. What should I do about it? Let's look first at what caused the problem. The pests you will be fighting are some (among many!) That will most likely cause problems in your garden.

Aphids

Aphids are children of garden pests. Even if there are no other creatures in your garden chewing the plants, they will probably end up with a few aphids. Look at the bottom of the leaves, most importantly the tender young leaves of delicate young plants and especially the tender young leaves of these. Small, pear-shaped polyps, and vocal.

Beetles

The beetles live up to the aphids on my list of least favorite garden visitors. They are of approximate head size and are dark brown or black; they look and act like fleas. As he gets closer, he jumps quite a distance. When you look a second time, they jump straight into the factory where they were having fun. They eat small holes in the leaves, especially the delicate leaves of young plants.

Fleas

Fleas like to walk on grassy places, in piles of old leaves, in shards of organic debris that accumulate around gardens. It is less and less likely that crows will find their tanks if they are not located near their places. Keep containers away from weeds and organic waste. Containers at least two feet from the ground are easier to maintain and less welcome for fleas.

Cabbage worms

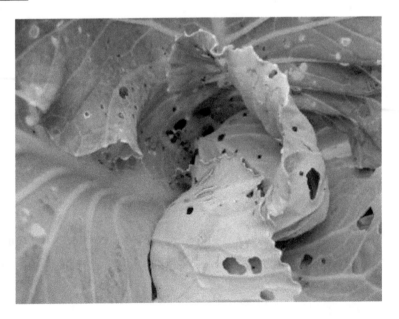

Cabbage worms are green, ideal for hiding in green plants, and are about an inch long. There are similar creatures, also green, called onion onions. If you are long and green and eat cabbage or broccoli, then you are a bad guy, and you would be better off not being there.

Potato beetles

Even if you don't grow potatoes, this is likely to happen to you. In a fairer world, this pest can well be called the Colorado potato beetle. Given its characteristics, Colorado beetle would eat eggplant leaves before those potatoes. And if the need arises, other members of this family will be eaten, including tomatoes and peppers.

Cucumber bugs

Small (1/3 inch) and narrow, the cucumber is available in two versions, both with yellow wings, but one with black stripes and the other with black spots. (They are known as striped cucumber and bug cucumber.) Although mostly found on their namesake plants, cucumber beetles also eat melons, zucchini, pumpkins, and sometimes beans and sweet corn. They also carry a bacterial vein, which can do even more damage than their diet.

Control. Mulch in rows will prevent bugs from finding plants. (Remove the lids two hours in the morning twice a week after the flowers appear to allow pollination.) Use a portable vacuum cleaner to vacuum the bugs and immediately vacuum with a vacuum cleaner in a bag to keep insects out.

Earwigs

About 6 inches long, brown, not very wide, and with tactile tweezers on the tip of the tail, the earlobe appears like a beneficial insect, not a plague in many insect books. Earwigs feed on pests of slow, sluggish bodies, such as aphids and larvae of various insects; They also help break down the decaying organic matter they like to live in. This is good news. Unfortunately, ear lice also have an appetite for young delicate garden plants; They can decimate seedlings of beans, cabbage, celery, carrots, broccoli, and marigold.

Control. If earrings become outlaws in my garden and eat my bean seedlings instead of the aphids I want to eat, what should I do? Catch them, then kill them by throwing them in the soap opera. How to catch them? Earwigs are nocturnal: they feed at night and hide in damp and dark places during the day. To catch them, plan damp, dark places - damp or rolled newspapers or sheets of cardboard on the floor are good options.

Drainage

When there isn't enough drainage in a pot, the soil is going to become waterlogged, and the roots of the plant will rot. This causes the plant to die. It's like having a bad heart.

The bad news is that most of the pots sold commercially do not have enough drainage. You can increase the drainage by drilling, carving, or punching larger holes into the container, but sometimes it's just easier to purchase a pot that has enough drainage. The minimum size for a drainage hole is around ½" in diameter for a small or medium-sized pot. For a larger container, look for a drainage hole that's an inch in diameter.

It is also a complete myth that adding pot shards, gravel, or stones to the bottom of the pot will increase drained. Some believe that if you do this, you don't need drainage holes at all. Unless you're very attentive and you're able to water perfectly, you're going to need holes in the pot. Also, if it rains and the pots are exposed to the rain, then they're going to need holes.

How to Protect Your Plants

Containers that have once been rich in color and foliage tend to fade and fail, gradually becoming worn out as the midsummer begins to roll in. As the temperatures start to rise, pretty blossoms and fleshy leaves start to wither and disappear. Fortunately, with proper care, your containers can flourish with vibrant health all summer.

There are crucial steps below that can be taken to create and maintain a brilliant display all through summer:

The first step towards having a healthy container is selecting the correct size of the pot, which is determined by different factors. Choosing a small planter with crowded roots will result in less water, oxygen, and nutrients available to the roots, and all these are important for their healthy growth.

On the other hand, when containers are too big, they will result in having excess moisture in the soil, thereby cutting off oxygen and eventually drowning the roots. Also, planters that have too much space with moist soil will help in solving most plant problems.

In a situation where the recommended spacing is ten to twelve inches, for example, you will make sure the plants are about six to eight inches apart. Generally, if their average growth is about ten to 12 inches tall, you should opt for a pot that is nearly half the size or width of around six to eight inches. In the case of plants that grow between 24 to 36 inches tall, you will need a larger container of about 24 inches in diameter. Also, ensure your pot is composed of drainage holes with the required material below it to enable excess water are flowing out smoothly.

It is also advisable to invert a smaller plastic pot over the drainage holes if adding more weight is an issue. There has also been some controversy as regards styrene from Styrofoam leeching into edibles. It was concluded that the low levels of styrene that are found in packaged food are due to the leaching that comes from the polystyrene containers in which they were packed. It is therefore recommended to make use of gravel, pieces of broken pottery, pebbles, nutshells, sticks, pinecones, or coffees as your drainage.

Also, note that container plants don't like their roots sitting in water. It will result in a wet root environment that will cause most bedding plants to sulk and have low growth. They can also cause the roots to rot, which makes planters inconvenient.

Drainage is also required to help provide your potted roots with adequate aeration. Because without this, and it will be hard for them to breathe and get easy access to oxygen.

Conclusion

Growing vegetables in containers, I believe, is becoming more popular, especially amongst city-dwellers who do not have acres of land to work, but perhaps have a balcony or terrace at their disposal.

I hope that this book has provided you enough knowledge and understanding of how Vegetable Container Gardening works. Plants need sunlight and water to grow. But they also need soil. If you recall, soil anchors the plants, so they don't fall over or blow away. But it also provides the nutrients and resources they need to grow. Plants need water and energy from sunlight to make their food. This process is called photosynthesis. With photosynthesis, plants turn water and nutrients into sugar. They use this sugar to grow big, but they also use it to make vegetables.

Many of the vegetables in your garden are not vegetables at all. They are true fruits! Fruits contain the seeds of the plant. From these seeds, a new plant will grow. So we benefit from eating fruits and vegetables. The plants benefit because we will plant, save, or spread their seeds. In this way, we help each other.

Before the plants make the seeds, though, do you remember what needs to happen to their flowers? That's right; they need to be fertilized. Fertilization means the flowers have what they need to make seeds. And to be fertilized, they first have to be pollinated! Different flowering plants do this in different ways. All of them need to move pollen from one flower to another. Some of them use the wind to do this. Others need help from special insects like bees. Those insects are called pollinators.

Plants need containers that are big enough for them to grow. Plants also need enough water - but not too much! If they do not have enough water, they will wilt and die. But if the soil becomes too full of water, the plants will not be able to get air, and they will drown. So, it is also very important to have good soil. You want soil that will keep some water, but that will also drain well.

I hope throughout the course; you have become excited about the unlimited possibilities of vegetable container gardening. Here are an edible hobby and pastime that offers you creativity for your expressions as well as food for your table.

Although this guide is designed for beginning gardeners starting their adventure into the land of vegetable container gardening, all of the information you just read is beneficial to any gardener regardless of age or experience. Now you know just how simple it can be to grow your edibles in the middle of city living – even if you have no yard or traditional gardening space.

Container planting is going to have a series of ups and downs associated with it. You need to ensure that you keep pushing forward and learning from your mistakes. That way, you end up expanding your knowledge and improving the overall results that you have in the garden. Remember, even experts had to start with very little knowledge in the garden.

There are many secrets to successful container gardening that the novice gardener may want to keep in mind. This form of gardening is very different from traditional gardening, especially since you must supply soil and nutrients on a routine basis for the plant. Even watering is a little more complex because there is no room for runoff, rather it soaks through, and this causes the ground to remain moist at all times.

With these tips, you should find that you are going to be better off in the garden. It is important to keep in mind that for many of these tips, it will help you to plan things out and to consider the layout of your garden in advance. Perhaps most importantly, it will be important that you do not give up on your first try. While these tips can increase your chances of success in the garden, it does not mean you will have instant success overnight. However, if you keep each tip in mind and use them to help improve the results that you have, in time, you should find that you do end up with a beautiful vegetable garden that you can be proud of.

Within you is the ability to grow a thriving gardener successfully. Make sure you take the time to nurture that individual and do all you can to grow vegetables that you love within containers that you have around your home. With a little fertilizer, quality soil and the right pots as mentioned in these tips, you are going to end up with a garden that you will love, and it will be one that all of your friends talk about for years to come.

By now, you will agree that it's quite easy to plant the vegetable of your choice at home by simply following the simple steps highlighted in this book. Understanding and practicing all the steps of planting your vegetable is a key to improved health as vegetables have lots of health benefits.

CPSIA information can be obtained
at www.ICGtesting.com
Printed in the USA
LVHW061537151020
668886LV00011B/333

9 781801 090865